THE BLUE MARBLE GAZETTEER

the
Blue Marble
GAZETTEER

David K. Leff

WAYFARER BOOKS

BERKSHIRE MOUNTAINS, MASS.

WAYFARER BOOKS

WWW.WAYFARERBOOKS.ORG

© 2022 TEXT BY DAVID K. LEFF

All Rights Reserved
Published in 2022 by Wayfarer Books
Cover Design and Interior Design by Leslie M. Browning
Cover Image: © Gael Gaborel
Interior Front Cover: © NASA
Interior Back Cover: © USGS
TRADE PAPERBACK 978-1-956368-17-8
HARDCOVER 978-1-956368-16-1

10 9 8 7 6 5 4 3 2 1

Look for our titles in paperback, ebook, and audiobook wherever books are sold. Wholesale offerings for retailers available through Ingram.

Wayfarer Books is committed to ecological stewardship. We greatly value the natural environment and invest in environmental conservation. For each book purchased in our online store we plant one tree.

ALSO BY THE AUTHOR

Echoes from Walden

New England Nature

Doppelgänger

The Breach

Terranexus

Canoing Main's Legendary Allagash

Maple Sugaring

Finding the Last Hungry Heart

Tinker's Damn

Hidden in Plain Sight

The Last Undiscovered Place

Deep Travel

The Price of Water

Death of Field

Acknowledgments

The author and publisher wish to express their grateful acknowledgment to the following publications in which these poems (some in earlier versions) first appeared or will appear: *Appalachia* ("Alpine Garden," "The Traveler," "Scrambling Toward Pomola"); *Connecticut River Review* ("Flea Market"); *Hartford Courant* ("Paintbrush and Rifle," "Skim Milk Sky," "Sleeping Giant," "Spring in the Ancient Burying Ground"); *Northern Woodlands* ("Snow Angels"); *Naugatuck River Review* ("Turkey Hunting"); *Today's American Catholic* ("Brook Foam", "Coronavirus Spring at Hammonasset Beach," "Frog Run," "Orb Weaver); *Your Daily Poem* ("Day of the Peepers," "Dreaming Norman Rockwell"). "Glass House" first appeared in the author's *Depth of Field* collection (Antrim House, 2010).

The author wishes to thank publisher and book designer extraordinaire Leslie M. Browning, his friends Amy Nawrocki and Eric Lehman for energetic discussions that helped inspire many of these poems, and former Connecticut state poet laureate Margaret Gibson for her insightful comments. Deepest gratitude to Kevin Dix who created the wonderful map included in this volume. Most of all, the author thanks his wife, Mary C. Fletcher, for her patient reading, rereading, and re-rereading of these poems.

contents

I. Cracks in the Glass

3   Glass House

5   Birdsong

7   Race to the Anthropocene

9   Texture of Silence

II. Shore & River

13   On the Beach

15   Last of the Real Norwalk Lobstermen

18   Coronavirus Spring at Hammonasset Beach

20   Rivertops

22   River Mussels

24   Brook Foam

25   Gone with the Flow

III. Sky

29   Light is Time

31   Cloudspotting

33   Broken Rainbow

35   Skim Milk Sky

IV. Roots & Branches

41   Snowshoes

43   Spruce Cathedral in Winter

45   Sumac in Winter

46   Standing Deadwood

48   Frost's Last Orchard

50   Lost Apples

53   Cedars: A Cautionary Tale

V. Peaks & Ridges

59   Higher Mountains to Climb

61   Alpine Garden

63   Scrambling Toward Pomola

66   The Traveler

68   Sleeping Giant

71   Finding Great Mountain Forest

VI. Other Lives

85   Snow Angels

87   Barred Owl

88   Day of the Peepers

89   Fox

91   Orb Weaver

92   Lepidoptera Opera

94   Winged Dusk

95   Turkey Hunting

98   Counting Crows

VII. Quotidian Errands

103   Garden

104   House Painting

106   Lawn Mowing

107   Supermarket Magic

110   Carotid Artery

112   Junk Drawer

114   Flea Market

116   Carolina Rocker

118   Anniversary at Equinox

119   Photographic Memory

120   Dreaming Norman Rockwell

VIII. Neighborhood

125   Around the Block

IX. Confluences

147   Frog Run

149   Trash Blossoms

150   Sidewalk Alive

151   Paintbrush and Rifle

152   Thoreau's Cairn

153   Life on Stone

154   Spring in the Ancient Burying Ground

157   Cicadas at Sixty

158   Finding Heaven

159   Instructions for a Funeral

About the author

About the press

I. Cracks in the Glass

One of the penalties of an ecological
education is that one lives alone in a world of wounds.

—*Aldo Leopold, A Sand County Almanac*

Glass House

Hunkered deep, every breath a strangled effort in January's
icy squeeze, I duck into the greenhouse for a quick dip
into summer. Smothered in womb-soft humidity, muscles
slacken and my defrosted mind wanders a jungled riot
of vegetable life thick with soil scents and respiring plants.

I could live forever in this indoor tropical island paradise
of rubber plants, cacao trees, lacy ferns and tendril-grasping
vines from the endless Augusts of Africa, Indonesia,
and South America. Seduced by perpetual green, I've
fallen for the alluring lips of glossy, crayon-colored orchids.

Thin light penetrating this crystal tent pours from sky
the color of frayed jeans. Flimsy glazing and furnaces
gobbling fossil fuel keep this artificial world refulgent
and sotted with photosynthesis when periodic arctics press
on the panes of a fragile fallacy.

I know about people living in glass houses, an evaporating

ozone layer, countless cars idling at stoplights and my

doctor's melanoma warnings. A lingering adolescence

looks for a rock: "break glass in emergency," school alarms

once instructed. Then I remember the cobwebby blue orb

captured in Apollo 8's earthrise and imagine

the greenhouse floating in space.

Birdsong

Nearly one-third of the wild birds in the United States
and Canada have vanished since 1970.
    —Fitzpatrick & Marra, *The New York Times*, 9/19/2019

I awaken to ghost birds,

my ears ringing with dawn choruses past—

robins, finches, warblers, thrushes, and wrens

erupting in melodies so loud and full I could not think,

my mind carried on a freshet of sound.

This morning is no silent spring,

but a season muffled, slowly choked of breath,

a boisterous choir fading to an ensemble

of sweet chirps and whistles,

not the wall of sound I heard as a boy.

Connecting earth, air and water,

wings and hollow bones morph to totems, portents.

Is there freedom or courage without eagles,

mystery absent owls peering into darkness,

peace and healing minus the grace of cranes?

I need no homing pigeons

when hushed birdsong augurs anxiety and awe,

messages me on the planet's health.

Must every feathered thing be a canary,

every backyard, street corner and hilltop a coal mine?

Race to the Anthropocene

My heart has little left for fear of living.
Time is broken,
an accelerating geological future-shock
convulsing the planet, triumph
of invention over biology.

September's warmth bleeds
into October, and I watch March
steal April's flowers as internal
combustion explodes in suicide
corrupting even the winds.

I'm witness to wildness tamed,
soil husbanded out of existence
with a final crop of pavement—
forest to dairy farm
to golf course and shopping plaza.

The Holocene is dead,
the slow unfolding of epochs
deranged by time-lapsed human-tectonic
change, wheels spinning too fast
for the living world.

Still, I believe in beaver dams,
haunting loon tremolos and wails,
the courage of turtles surviving since
Triassic times, multigenerational
migrations of monarchs.

With dread resisting awe,
I hope against hope
for creative dreaming and awakening
before the turning point
beyond which there is no return.

Texture of Silence

A lichen patched boulder is the texture
of silence I long to emulate. I want to melt
into the landscape, forget the surveyor
and yield to the survey like oaks and pines,
sparkling schist, red sandstone.

I yearn to be camouflaged, an unseen
sensation like wind on my cheek, or the stream
chattering in my ears. Distilled to an essence,
I'd find a place where prayers expand
forever, like the air I breathe.

II. Shore & River

The edge of the sea is a strange and beautiful place.
—*Rachel Carson, The Edge of the Sea*

On the Beach

Ebb tide, air rich with scents of salted
decay, the rot and recycling of life.
Sea rushes to shore with rhythmic pulses,
and I feel the stroke of seawater within,
my heart pumping to an endless wave-beat.

Water slides up the beach, seeps back
and returns again and again, a cadence
of inhale and exhale soothing the body
but exciting my mind to wander.

Tide pool to desiccated wrack line
ajumble with broken life is the distance
from birth to grave, but I see only the sun's
hide-and-seek with clouds, wind tickling water.

By the moon's irresistible, silent tow
the sea kisses the high dried debris twice
daily. Its force tugs on my bones,
reptilian brain dumbly possessed.

Restless as the sea, I'm always pushing
and pulling back. Feeling in my fingers
the waves raking sand, I'm drunk
with salt spiced over-ripeness.

I envy angel-winged gulls floating,
wheeling on breezes, drifting backward,
strolling the water's edge, chancing on
shellfish, putrid carcasses, and human detritus,
seizing advantage on the living fringe.

Last of the Real Norwalk Lobstermen

Henry grabs the buoy with a boat hook,
wraps the line on a winch and hauls a seven
pot trawl, bits of seaweed and mud
flying off the rope. Large gloved hands
snatch wire cages as they surface

with a dripping splutter. Muscular,
with a creased, leathery face,
spindly chicken legs in short pants,
and bulging biceps, he's Popeye escaped
from cartoons and comic strips, shaped

by seventy-five years of sun, wind,
salt and tides. Caught in the wire parlor,
several glossy, dark-olive lobsters scuttle
about like giant Jurassic insects.
Shorts and a few eggers, spider

crabs and a starfish go overboard
with a plop, the keepers tossed into
a tank of circulating seawater.
Looking out at clusters of colorful plastic
buoys like a field of floating flowers,

he points a finger: "Greedy sons-of-bitches,"
he says in a voice rising from low growl
to godly bellow, "some of these bastards
with a couple thousand pots aren't making
a living, they're doing a killing,

raping the resource." In a tattered orange
apron, Henry boasts about his new
Harley, cuts thick chunks of stinking,
oily mackerel, stuffing them into each
emptied trap, a "lobster's gourmet

fantasy." Years ago he was bar to bar
raising hell, igniting fights. Now
"everyone scrambles when they see
this old fuck coming," he says. "No telling
 what the SOB will do." Henry puts

the baited pots on the rail, slowly
piloting the boat forward, each one
falling with a rhythmic splash, quickly
disappearing beneath sun-sparkled green water.
"There are no laws," he explains, "just

restrictions on peoples' lives."
But he keeps close to the pulse,
tying up his thirty-six-footer each
night beside the police boat. Hosing
mud, fish oil and debris off the deck,

he guides the boat around a maze of red,
blue, and purple buoys. "It's a pirate
business," he says. "Pricks soaking
pots just to hold ground when fishing
sucks, sabotaging boats, cutting lines."

Henry fished until lobsters faded
in warming Long Island Sound waters.
A force of nature, he held on until Nature
gave out. "Never pray for me," he'd laugh.
"No one gets outta here alive."

Coronavirus Spring at Hammonasset Beach

First day of spring, my wife and I walk
the beach under a milky, pearlescent sky,
the sea quiescent, chalky like the inside
of an oyster shell. In the distance,
water fades to air at a ghostly horizon.

Strangely, we find comfort
in spicy salt and rancid fish scents,
circling gulls calling shrilly, waves
lapping at sand that gives way underfoot.

Walkers of all ages and complexions
pass us, but repel
like common-pole magnets
in these uncertain Coronavirus days.

As if there's nothing to fear,
children build castles for tides to devour,
a couple toss a football, and two teen
girls dance wildly to music only they hear.

Bearded, wearing a ballcap, holding
a wooden staff, a man stops and smiles.
"Nice day for the world to end,"
he chuckles slyly. "I won't repent."

I've imagined ice, fire and thunder,
yet the last day in billions of years,
when the sun's corona
flares-out, may be quiet like today.

Just as when the twin towers fell
in flames and dust, Mary and I find solace
by the sea which birthed all life.
In centrifugal times we're drawn to water,
perhaps searching for a second chance.

Rivertops

I follow brooks upgradient
to heights quite low, sources
of flowing water braided of springs,
vernal pools, seeps and swamps

where streams marry gravity,
rush seaward. It's not so simple
as tracing a drop falling on a slope,
or seeking moisture sweating

from humus, percolating
in pockets of sand and gravel,
a maze of bedrock fractures,
or weeping from mists shredded

on uneven ground. But fruitless
searches are rewarded by serendipitous
finds—a muscular oak
centuries old, bear caves, bobcat scat,

a glacially sculpted ledge upholstered

in iridescent moss and lichen rosettes.

We hunger for beginnings, pray

for sources, long for essences, the birth

of purity, beauty and power,

some incipient Mississippi, Nile or Amazon.

But where you go depends on your map

in a Rand-McNally world dotted

with cities and towns, bound

by varicose networks of watercourses

and roads, consigning rivertops to cloud-

built cartographies awaiting discovery.

River Mussels

The name of a thing may easily
be more than the thing itself to me.
                    —H. D. Thoreau

heelsplitter, tidewater mucket, shinyrayed

pocketbook, oval pigtoe, wartyback

Blind, sedentary and soundless, names

of these living rocks are the music

of human imagination, spell

primal wonder in wild creatures.

pearlshell, dwarf wedgemussel, alewife floater,

eastern elliptio, sheepnose, pistolgrip

Glossy amber to greenish brown,

these ovoid cobbles with concentric

calcium rings hide beneath currents,

filter detritus and bacteria, stabilize

streambeds, feed muskrats, herons, and otters.

triangle floater, fat threeridge, purple

bankclimber, monkey face, elephant ear

Secret sentinels of clean water,

we smother them with poisoned sediments,

drown them with dams, confident

that what we don't see can't help us.

Brook Foam

—for Jody Bronson, woodsman

Rushing in a tea-tinted freshet,

McMullen Brook draws me downstream

as it winds around rocks,

slides over logs, strains

through tangles of low hanging branches

until slowed in a deep,

swirling dark eddy where the water

is whipped to a beehive of foamy meringue.

Dizzily it twirls, a rotisserie of tiny

rotting leaf particles and dying

algae whisked to a froth. I see a pirouetting dancer,

spinning cotton candy, and my childhood top

all collapsed into a hypnotic

clockwork of accelerating time where invisible

briefly becomes visible in a whirlpool

churning with precious decay.

Gone with the Flow

I stand stone still on the bank, letting the river
move for us both. My mind meanders
from rock-riffled shallows to a dark, waxy
pool at my feet. How odd
to be mesmerized by mere physics of runoff.

My frenetic world endlessly nags
with ideas and doings, but the river soothes
and calms by its own relentless motion.
I hardly recognize myself, caught
in stasis, letting water do the work.

The river is inside me. I am the river.

Looking down, my mirrored face looks up,
floating among clouds and ragged
overhanging branches like a photoshopped collage.
Breezes stir the water, massage my image
from soft impressionism to surreal distortion.

I'm drowning in a hydrology of random
dreams, part of the current, feeling
an irresistible stream of consciousness
flow over cobbles and gravel.
I take a few dips in the river, but never get wet.

III. Sky

It is a very strange thing how little in general people know about the sky.
—*John Ruskin, Modern Painters*

Light is Time

Light is time made visible,
sunshine a measure of my days,
moons marking months,
stars pulsing with years.

I crave the now,
lean into the future
like a headwind, but live
in the past's receding light.

Daylight is over eight
minutes late from the sun,
moonshine just a mirrored shimmer,
and four long years must pass

to feel the freshest starlight
fall in luminous
after-dark rain.
Time will not be rushed,

so I find solace in a cyclical

world of days, months, and seasons

even as I crave an endless

string of years.

All is flowing photons,

a truth offering barely

enough lumens to expose tattered

edges of our darkest mysteries.

Cloudspotting

... to make the shifting clouds be what you please ...
    —*Coleridge*

I breathe the airy essence of clouds

as they shape my moods, kindle

longings, foment dreams, loosen ephemeral

Rorschach mists of imagination.

Gazing skyward, I see islands

in an azure ocean, cauliflowered mountains,

strands of silky angel's hair

or pewtered plains horizon to horizon

prophesizing wind, snow, rain, sun.

Lazily, I conjure floating elephants

and faces, a celestial eye, charging bear

morphing into spirals, a question

mark, chair, fish, tractor, and lightning bolt

as whimsy loosens memory.

Science speaks of cooling vapor,

of dust, water droplets or ice.

I summon dances of chaos

and complexity scattering and reflecting

light in a theater of internal weather

where I see what I will.

Broken Rainbow

And the waters prevailed and increased greatly upon the earth
  —*Genesis* 7:18

Rhythmic waves are my heartbeat,

blood chemistry, pulse

of breath, the pungent salt air

scented with my sweat.

Moody and restive, like me

the sea rages with fist-pounding

breakers, flattens in serene calm.

We arose from the ocean

and now call it back to us

with warming respirations from boilers

and engines melting glaciers,

mountainous icebergs and icecaps

of eternal winter dissolving

in saltwater sumps. Once frozen

worlds now unlocked swell relentless

tides, will devour homes and factories,

crash over walls, drown streets,

swallow bright green spartina

marshes and river mouths, form

islands from conifer covered mountains.

No rainbow promise can save us.

No ark is large enough.

Oceans eagerly return,

reclaim their ancient inland realms

as we struggle for new buoyancy.

Skim Milk Sky

—Historic Wildfires Rage in Western States
The New York Times, 9/10/20

Beneath hazy skies tinged skim-milk-blue,

I feel pressure, a weight

where New England's endless azure

September should lighten my steps.

Weirdly visible, air is soot-smudged from blazes

devouring California's homes and hillsides,

the sun's eye clouded by a smoky cataract.

A slight, acrid scent brings me back

to days cutting line with a Pulaski, spritzing hotspots

from a backpack tank, old stumps

burning like braziers, snags falling

and splintering, foliage crackling like foil

in long hours of sweat, heat, and adrenaline—

rushed heartbeats. Having witnessed the savage

hunger of flames, I envision charred wreckage

and broken lives in these soft flannel skies,

the sooty air filled with heaven's portion of forests

reduced to ragged shadows. Time's gradual click

plays tricks on human minds,

and slow-paced climate change seems a future

exceeding our grasp. I live in a digital age

that scoffs at ancients who augured with meteor

and eclipse, but by merely looking upward

into a cloudless monotony of gray, I know

we connect to California with every breath.

IV. Roots and Branches

A culture is no better than its woods.
—*W. H. Auden, "Bucolics"*

Snowshoes

The shoes remember the tree
in a straight-grained, strong frame
flexing step after step, the wood
slowly tempered by seasons well-watered
and dry, cold and sweltry.

The shoes embody the hand
and eye of the crafter—steam bent,
sanded smooth, lacquered
to a sheen, and woven in a complex
web of rawhide, time and skill.

The shoes imprint in soft
powder with waffled snow angel
feet. They crunch on icy crust.
Always they leave an ephemeral track
lodged longer in the mind than in nature.

The shoes invite imagination.
Conjuring animal totems from the woods,
they leave behind elongated
beavertail, oval bearpaw, narrow pickerel,
and swallowtail shapes.

The shoes know every step

among spruce and leafless yellow birch,

ground that's granular or mushy

like mashed potatoes, frozen streams,

and steep slopes to windswept summits.

The shoes harbor memories

that rush back with but a glance at a pair

of well-worn racquets. After last

breaths, they hold our deep winter secrets

just as the shoes remember the tree.

Spruce Cathedral in Winter

Even at noon light is thin and dim
among the towering Norway spruce
with dour downcast black-green branches,
at least seven stories tall, pointed
tops like rockets ready to launch.
I look up along trunks with brittle,
bony dead limbs to fragments of sky.

Despite a night's powdery snowfall,
the ground is only sugared in patches,
prismatic crystals slowly sifting
through a seine of stiff needles
in breezes swaying crowns,
but not felt below in this darkling
Mirkwood of lurking mystery.

Eight decades ago, the muscular
young men of Roosevelt's tree army
planted a few acres of sunlit field
in straight rows of tender, bare-root
seedlings, loosening grass-tangled soil
with spades and dibble bars for plants
whose survival seemed doubtful.

Long forgotten, the spruces now
stand like courthouse columns,
crowded in soldierly file, umbrellas
of crepuscular eternity. But I blink
and look again, and now they seem
slanted, arrayed in shifting
diagonal lines that shimmer and fade.

Perspective plays tricks
with my eyes, as the trunks lose
their rhythm, seem to trade space
with each other until I feel inside
a quickly shifting geometry,
a dizzying Escher-like maze
where one thing becomes another.

Not wild enough for nature,
defying a garden's tidy trim,
these trees make mischief with my mind.
Estranged from the ordinary
in an encrypted landscape, they await
saws, ice, or windthrow to renew cycles
of growth with moisture and light.

Sumac in Winter

Branched like a crazy candelabra
supporting crimson flame-shaped fruits,
staghorn sumac burns for months
but is not consumed. Conical bunches
of berries make snow whiter, sky richer.
On the year's altar, sacred
to the ceremony of the seasons,
they're memorial lights for the last day,
birthday candles for the first.
Growing at field edges and in waste
places, most of us don't notice the ruby glow.
Bluebirds, robins, and squirrels
know better, plucking at the jeweled lights
to keep their own fires burning.

Standing Deadwood

Sun silvered,

half rain rotted,

limbs broken,

bark sloughing,

an apartment tower

of unrepentant life.

Glossy lacquer top

and turkey tail fungi

cling like climbing holds

along the trunk—

softening, decomposing,

inviting insects.

Bark beetles inscribe

tunneled calligraphy,

carpenter ants carve hollows,

woodpeckers hammer

at a cafeteria of termites,

spiders, woodborers.

Wrens and bluebirds nest
in sapsucker or flicker-
chiseled holes. Raccoons,
owls, and squirrels
shelter in cavities
left by broken limbs.

Dead is beautiful
where hawks perch high
to spot mice and voles,
and timber slowly
decays to humus,
nourishing humanity.

Frost's Last Orchard

I am apple orchard.
    —Robert Frost, "Mending Wall"

I sat on Frost's porch,
looked across his meadow to distant
forested hills, and bit into an apple
purloined from trees he'd planted.

Gnarly, scabbed, rust spotted,
the tart, ugly fruit curled my tongue,
the reddish peel thick,
ivory flesh firm and satisfying.

The poet tended an orchard
wherever he lived, and after apple-picking
harvested poems blossoming
with rhyme, ripening to metaphor.

Could I taste
his stanzas, rhythms and diction?
Did his imagination press words
from fruit like cider?

Asters, goldenrod, and wild carrot
bloomed in tall grass
beneath split trunks and pecker-fretted,
lichen crusted branches.

Skeletal, twisted, wild for decades,
the trees cast thin shadows,
readied for hearth-side flames even
as sun-struck fruit hung like holiday ornaments.

With the poet's cumulus of white hair,
his granite-chiseled face,
the wizened trees seemed grown
in the octogenarian orchardist's image.

Frost never saw his saplings mature,
but on this warm, late September day
I savored his payment forward,
felt his longing for extension.

I imagined forbidden fruit
from the tree of poetic knowledge,
chewed a last savory mouthful,
and tossed the core into the woods.

Lost Apples

An apple seed doesn't grow a replica of the parent,
but only a rough facsimile.
    —Roger Yepsen, *Apples*

You won't find them among glossy

jewels of Red Delicious, Honeycrisp

and Granny Smith arrayed in pyramids

and orderly rows of the produce aisle

where eyes cheat the tongue,

prizing perfection in bright colors

and unblemished skin of mass-produced clones.

Gone is the juicy crunch of Pucker End,

Delaware Bottom, Stormproof, and Bachelor Blush.

Never again tangy sips from fresh pressed

mixes of Golden Wilding, Rough-and-Ready,

Lopside, and Black Michigan

consigned now to faded catalogs and books

in an afterlife of paper cemeteries

for the extinct and nearly so.

You might as well converse with the dead,

taste time itself, as bite into Bushwhacker,

Catface, Uncle Archy, or Front Door.

Like family photos of the departed,

they pose in formal paintings—

round, conical, oblong—yellow with blush,

freckled reds, waxy greens.

We know both smart and bad apples,

polishers rotten to the core,

and the apples of our eyes.

There's Schoolfield for the teacher

as American as pie, and Ladies Eardrop

or sweet Ferris Wheel to keep doctors away.

How do we like them apples

when only little green ones are heaven sent?

Names tell stories— Keep Forever, Early Breakfast,

Craven's Winter—since we are fated

to become what we eat. We fill stomachs,

slake thirsts, brains abuzz with applejack

for service as vectors scattering

trees across the globe even as we still

hunger for a last bite at Eden's forbidden fruits.

Brown, hard, bitter and buried deep within,

seeds harbor secrets, a wild genetic chaos

little regarding pedigree.

Double helix of hope and uncertainty,

crapshoot of anxiety and serendipity,

chance saplings like Fail Never,

Sweet-Seek-No-Further, or Great Unknown

tempt truth with pips never growing true to type.

Cedars: A Cautionary Tale

In the shadow of towering oaks
I find islands of skeletal cedars,
years ago drowned in shade, their bony
branches hugging ruddy brown trunks
and reaching upward
in supplication to long lost light.

Clustered as if in conversation
beside a mossy stone wall,
they pioneered a rock-muscled hillside
pasture now grown to forest
after Jerseys and Holsteins climbed
no more to this windswept knob of wild grasses.

Once tenacious flames of green,
they witnessed the economics of dairy,
succession of trees, tourist camera clicks
capturing the picturesque,
while kinglets, grosbeaks, and waxwings
feasted on blue-black berries.

Equal to living centuries, they stood
but decades in slowly shifting circumstances
as stems of oak, black birch and hickory
quietly swallowed them in rising tides
of twilight, leaving once evergreen spires
barren in forever winter.

V. Peaks & Ridges

A people who climb the ridges . . .
who enter the forest and scale the peaks . . .
will give the country some of the indomitable spirit of the mountains.
—**William O. Douglas**, *Of Men and Mountains*

Higher Mountains to Climb

Ten dead on Everest by mid-May.
Bodies frozen, oxygen starved,
faces sunburned, dreams stillborn.

Lines rivaling DMV on a bad day
or the bank at closing,
the grocery register before a holiday.

Jumbles of oxygen bottles,
ripped tents, broken ladders, cans,
wrappers, and crap pile up in snow.

Muscle, ego, money, and gear
can't get you where Norgay
buried sweets and Hillary a crucifix.

Tallest but hardly most remote,
wild, or technically difficult,
the name always seduces.

Thirty years after his conquest,
I had a moment with the man who shared
first on the ultimate summit.

Gangling, with a glacially carved,
ruddy face, he smiled warmly.
"Call me Ed," he said softly.

I imagined a titan in goggles, boots,
and parka, but he might have been happier
with his bees, a smoker and veil.

As if over a pint and shepherd's pie
at a pub, we talked of building hospitals
and schools for Nepal's people.

He had higher mountains to climb,
and urged me to come with him,
scaling peaks far above the clouds.

Alpine Garden

a plateau on Mt. Washington

Wind ripples through rock
studded grasses, tousles my hair, drives
dirigible cumulus across a blue sea.

The massive summit cone of broken talus
looms on one side; craggy, muscular ravines,
a horizon of peaks and ridges on the other.

Exposed in a gray, bouldery vastness,
breathless from climbing, chilled by sweat,
I brave sunlight that stings my eyes, sears

my neck as I hopscotch rocks, pockets
of frilly Lapland rosebay blossoms.
Afoot where life feels thin, I spot

fallen stars of diapensia flourishing
in a green firmament, moss campion
firing pink in sheltered nooks.

Ambushed by drying wind, baked in sun,

squeezed in frozen ground half the year,

frail blossoms thrive where I'm a tourist.

Bent low, I sniff alpine azaleas

where boot-soles can kill, and missteps

at the edge have a long afterlife.

Scrambling Toward Pomola

Pomola is always angry with those
who climb to the summit of Ktaadn.
    —H.D. Thoreau

I

I don't belong, and that's why I'm here.

One footstep, one handhold at a time,

each move a thought as I

climb and crawl over chunks of fractured

rock narrow as a couple feet, a dizzying

abyss of 1,500 to either side.

Only August, but it feels November,

my ears burning with cold and wind-chatter.

Swirling clouds pass so fast, the forest far below

flickers with shadows like an old-time film,

a rucked green tarp dotted with irregular lakes

gleaming like broken mirrors.

I'm a trespasser. Only rosettes of gray-green

lichen know what it takes to live here—

tattoos on stone,

hieroglyphs warning the entrance

to a pharaoh's tomb. I pause for breath, heart

in mouth, a sip of water stings like whiskey.

II

Balancing, a highwire act, dancing

in sudden gusts on Katahdin's

Knife Edge, I scramble toward Pomola,

conical pile of busted-up granite, avenging

Penobscot guardian spirit—moose head,

human body, eagle wings and feet.

I'm not supposed to believe,

but as I creep closer, sometimes on hands

and knees in seeming supplication,

daring the uneven edge,

his claws rake my back and face with wind.

Slowly, slowly I go in awe and trepidation.

I'm clambering over the planet's

backbone, a gauntlet whose creation seems rough,

unfinished. Pomola devours my energy

in great gulps, leaves me exhausted, cramped.

Could the ancient god still hold sway?

Should I expect signs and wonders?

Death here is not merely hypothetical, so I'm torn

between exhilaration and dread, my life as tenuous

as my grip on rock. Danger is more than metaphorical,

and far from metaphysical fictions of ordinary

time and daily routine. Clouds cross the ridge,

a world disappears, and suddenly exists again.

III

After four decades, I return often in a Brigadoon

of mind, a shadow hike in Pomola's shadow.

Pilgrimage became vision quest when life

was a query to querulous fortune, just a guess.

Conquest grew less about summits than self,

and I climb because I'm here, not because it's there.

Katahdin's immortal as anything I'll ever

know despite the slow ebb

by an eternity of erosion. But, Pomola's

mysteries grow since the play of mind whets

a sharper edge than any I could climb,

and the high point lies far from the peak.

The Traveler

north of Katahdin

No trail atop the Traveler, so
in hot sun and a sharp breeze
I bushwhack thick krummholz
of stunted spruce, stumbling
in tangles of small, crooked trees
that grab legs, scratch arms.

Reaching the gray scree slope
of fractured rhyolite, hardened
remains of a long dead volcano,
I tiptoe from rock
to rock, the knobby summit
a few hundred feet above.

To one side, a flash
of white, and I walk to a scattering
of bleached moose bones—
skull gone, but a dozen ribs,
a couple femurs, scapula, broken
mandible, glistening pelvic bone.

Why had a moose strayed
so high, so far from food
and shelter? Driven mad
by brainworm? Seeking relief
from heat and blackflies?
A broken leg? Disease?

And why did I struggle up a mountain
of middling height without
peculiar features, rare views?
Skipping the peak, I kneel beside the bones,
picturing the lumbering animal
picking its awkward way up.

Now, forty years on, a femur
on my shelf at home haunts
with questions. And what of the old-time
woodsmen who named the mountain
that traveled with them
as they chased logs downstream?

Sleeping Giant

a traprock ridge near home

You were invisible as I watched my step
on tricky traprock, climbing along narrow
ravines thick with oak and beech, breathing hard
as I reached the ridge. Dazzled by valley,
city, and water views from your cliff-edge
chin and high hip, the notion of chest, arms
and legs seemed an extravagance,
a figment of metaphor. Turkey vultures
circled on thermals searching for delicious
death, but their graceful flight was all I knew.

Driving north from New Haven one afternoon,
I saw you, three miles from head to foot,
lying on your back and fast asleep, the clear
outline of your body exposing my Lilliputian
myopia, the failed reality of our relationship
when the trails brought me close among the hemlocks
and hardwoods, and along the jagged windswept
ledges where I imagined I knew you.

I now walk quietly, knowing that the spirit

Kiehtan drowsed you into deep, stony sleep for rowdy

behavior moving rivers, causing floods,

and gorging yourself on the people's oysters.

In this moment of soft spring air

it's as believable as the violent upwelling of molten

earth two hundred million years ago

and the tedious eons of cooling and erosion.

You've shown me there is more

than one way of looking, that one size never fits all.

A century ago, quarrymen exploded your head,

crushed stone and carted it away

to build the roads which bring me easily

into your colossal presence. My heart knows

they stopped for fear blasting would awaken

you in anger to uproot trees and rip up soil,

again altering the course of waters with the whole

country trembling at your laborious rise.

Slowly I climb the muscular, angular,

slope of your slumbering body. I feel your pine-

scented breath as I breathe. Your human shape

has kept these woods, left you protector

of pileated woodpeckers, salamanders, wood frogs,

Christmas fern, foxes, deer, and flowers

from bloodroot in March to September's asters.

Rest well, snooze away as awe and wonder awaken

a hiker's ordinary days and keep you alive

in a landscape created in our own image.

Finding Great Mountain Forest

a woodland in Connecticut

For myself, I live by the leaves.
  —*Wallace Stevens*

I

Never alone in the forest,

trees watch, listen, absorb my intentions

and dreams as easily as exhaled breath.

Garrulous sylvan dialects speak to me

in growth habits and habitat alchemized

by a grammar of carbon dioxide, sunshine, rain,

and soil that hold in dendritic vessels of carbon,

an idiom stretching the soul.

Under summer's rippling leaves

or crosshatched bare branches lined with snow,

I seek a world of anomaly and variability

where nothing is even, precisely angled or level.

Sugar maples lean and twist in hunger for light,

the burnt-potato-chip bark of black cherry

bulges with knobby burls,

yellow birch roots snake around rocks

like arthritic fingers, and racoons homestead
in oak hollows left by ice-storm severed limbs.

Daypack stuffed with water bottle
and sandwich, matches, compass, first aid kit,
fishing line, maybe a sweatshirt,
I also carry Pooh's Hundred Acre Wood,
Schwartzwald mysteries, Eden's forbidden branches.
I roam where Frost's swinging birches
are lit to skeletal x-rays, and saplings
seeded from Yggdrasil,
the grand ash connecting worlds,
might well have rooted.
Everyone brings trees to the forest.

In standing timber I recall
pine clapboards, cherry tables,
hickory axe handles and cedar pencils
that frame my days, the heart
of what's crooked and irregular
milled into objects simple, smooth and uniform.
Even embalmed with stains and varnish,
the grain of living growth urges
me to look up into twig networks,
roadmaps of possibilities against the sky.

II

Bathed in April morning moonrise,

nasal buzzing breaks stillness

as a timberdoodle rises in twirling spirals,

twittering above a field

of matted grass, sky-dances for a mate

in milky twilight,

dropping like feathered stone

and rising again.

I want to dance.

Wandering a hummocky, dimly lit

red spruce swamp, lonely woodwind

hermit thrush whistles

penetrate tangles of branches

and the heart's own thickets, soundtrack

in dark, dour conifer silence.

I want to sing.

A porcupine lazes like a day-drunk

on an August oak branch.

The forest works on me until

it is within, until I sprout quills, until

I want to sleep off midday heat among the leaves.

On an old clearcut's ragged edge
I forage raspberries until a bear
and cub crash brambles, flies
buzzing, black coats shimmering
even under overcast,
pink tongues vacuuming knubby fruit.
I want to eat from the forest.

Acorn to oak, oak to acorn
and browsing deer, a shotgun slug
rockets over fallen acorns,
evolves to grilled venison, a climax of acorns.
Hunters become acorns,
gather stories as if collecting acorns,
while leaflitter-tossed root-ends crack
acorn shells, burrow into soil, sprouting oaks.
I want to grow in the forest.

I wait to ripen as a raven's metallic croak,
well-palmed moose antlers,
bobcat eyes, a green frog's banjo twang,
cattail flower fluff, the booming of icebound
Wapato Pond, a shaggy hickory trunk
dressed like rough-cut woodsmen grown to trees.
I want to be of the forest.

III

Boulders set boundaries in boundless

acres where property divisions, rhumb-lines

and town borders are slowly absorbed.

Trees swallow old farmsteads, cellar holes,

fields and kitchen gardens, leaving only

lichen crusted stonewalls and names on maps

—Chattleton, Dorman, Mansfield.

Tumbling froth from ledge to rock,

Brown Brook shouts truth to winds

raking hemlock tops, strobing light

on ground where shadows dawdle at noon.

Phantom sluiceways, broken dams,

a few rusted nails and metal scraps

recall water as power

turning gears and leather belts for wolf-toothed

saws rough-cutting lumber

still embedded in old buildings or long rotted away.

Flattened circles of blackened earth

remember smudgy fires

from mounds of moss-covered cordwood slowly

distilled to carbon, to charcoal

feeding iron forges for railcar wheels,

axe heads and cannonballs.

Sooty-faced souls of sleep-deprived colliers

linger as dark, shadowy ghosts

among large multi-trunked trees they once coppiced.

In this afterlife of past presences,

time's membrane is porous and translucent.

Centuries are written in soil horizons

and concentric tree rings.

And human memory haunts these woods

where a holy man prayed and fed birds from a cave,

Lt. Thorson's P-40 Tomahawk crashed

to explosions of dirt and stone,

and Jack's Rock drank blood in a brawl over charcoal.

Collapsing cellar holes and overgrown

Meekertown cemetery embrace forgotten lives

a quick crow-flight from a grand mansion long gone

where Goodnow's name lingers on maps.

The forest sponges stories like carbon dioxide.

They remain written on the land

in a Braille palimpsest clear as glacial

scratches on granite ledges.

IV

Hard and bony, too mean for farming,

iron masters left worthless, eroded brushland

when blasts went out and furnaces cold.

Sold cheap, Boone and Crockett Club

Walcott and Childs imagined rockbound slopes

and scarred lowlands healed with towering oak,

hickory, beech, and hemlock sheltering resurgent deer,

turkey, bear, and bobcat. They moved earth and stone,

turning swamps to ponds where black and wood

duck, great blue heron, merganser and bittern

found luminous oases to feed and raise young.

Cash from carbon combustion spinning dynamos,

lighting homes by poles and wires fueled

purchase of parcel after parcel for almost a century.

Season after season, growth rings accrued

and crowns reached skyward.

Rescued by electric carbon exhalations,

thousands of woodland acres beckoned

to foresters, lumbermen, hikers and scientists.

Plantations of exotic conifers, scientific transects,

sawtimber plots, witch hazel harvests,

and sap tapped for syrup flourished beside beaver
meadows dotted with standing deadwood
enlivened with sapsuckers and woodpeckers
devouring ants, beetles, and termites
returning trees to soil.

Trees spread and thickened
for over seventy years on the watch
of foresters Kiefer, Russ, Bronson and Russ.
Listening to what the land whispered,
they harvested sawlogs and planted saplings,
pruned white pine, kept diaries of rising sap and leaf-out,
records of pond ice, return and departure of warblers,
bear and moose ramblings, bloom of trout lily, laurel,
goldenrod and aster. Measuring each inch of rain
or snow, capturing wind, heat and cold
with numbers and charts, they grew
on the forest and the forest in them.

Now the woods brace for freakish weather
as rising temperatures, longer droughts,
loitering heat waves, and intense bursts
of rainfall test resilience
in an ever-changing forest of transitory moods

where fungus reduces chestnut to shrubs,

emerald spangled borers perforate ash,

and wooly adelgid sucks the lifeblood from hemlock.

Locked up with public easements,

under long-term contract to harbor carbon

it was once worked to release,

the forest persists as it must,

provides dimensional lumber,

fuelwood, veneer and syrup,

teaches reindeer moss and box turtle economics,

sparks awe and wonder in all who enter.

V

Spicy sweetness like fresh-split red oak

grows with each step toward the water,

each crunch of leaves, each twig snap

under a popcorn cumulus sky.

Wind rippled Crissey Pond is a bright mirror,

a dish of leaf-rot releasing carbon

where sunfish, perch and bullhead feed

spirit and body with a monofilament tug

and a mouthful of fried-up flavor.

Slicing open stomachs to half-digested midges

and mosquitoes, or a tiny crayfish,
I know what I'm eating.

Water speaks to a chorus of frogs,
laps on rocks and mossy logs half-sunken.
Slapping at gnats and blackflies,
I watch insects seduced by pitcher plants,
drowned in tubular reddened lip-like leaves
full of nectar along the boggy shore.
Life is hunger and happening.

Crissey gathers light at dusk
until more luminous than darkening sky.
Seeking my reflection among trees and clouds,
I could swim and float in the heavens
as cool, damp air embraces.
Stars erupt like dust motes caught
in moonbeams, seeming closer,
more welcoming than any porchlight.

I'm a divining rod with ears, eyes, nose,
hand and tongue searching for something
that searches for me.

I willingly return home, yet part of me lives

here, cannot go back, a necessity of spirit

awaiting rediscovery of sylvan

magic within in an endless rush of life

where I am carbon absorbed,

spent, and absorbed again.

VI. Other Lives

Humanity is exalted not because we are so far above other creatures,
but because knowing them well elevates the very concept of life.
—*Edward O. Wilson, Biophilia*

Snow Angels

I

On my way to the woods, I watch
children on their backs in newly fallen
snow, arms and legs waving up
and down. Leaping to their feet,
sparkling with crystal dust, they look
down to find their angel, a white shadow.

I remember cold pressing on me like a hand
while looking into an endless arc of sky
as snow-colored clouds gave chase.
Now, I feel warmth from rising joy,
knowing these boys and girls will feel
the same into old age whenever they see
angelic impressions in fresh powder.

II

Beneath trees I find scratched
circles, lines and angles drawn
by desiccated plant stalks and seedhead
plumes driven by the wind's insatiable

whim, crypto-writing in language
I don't understand, but ache to learn.

I follow white-footed mouse tracks,
tiny four-print, bounding impressions
connected by tail-dragged lines
until they abruptly end at a broad, wing-
and-tail feathered snow angel
whose message is clear, as indelible
as a child's ephemeral imprints.

Barred Owl

Vigilant, sphinx-like, perched
high among spruce branches,
solemn searchlight brown eyes
pierce viscous darkness for barely
visible frogs, crayfish, voles and snakes.

Hoohoo-hoohoo, hoohoo-hooohooooaw
haunts the night air, draws me deep
into shadowy woods. "Who cooks for you,
who cooks for you-all" sounds mysterious,
profound. Who's in my kitchen, I wonder.

Hard wired instinct of muscle and feathers,
owls are sovereign over sage mnemonics.
We've conflated concentration
with intuition, visual acuity with wisdom,
wondering why we aren't any wiser.

Day of the Peepers

Risen from half frozen muck,
peepers give voice to awakening soil,
chanting a sharp, piping whistle.

I hear a thousand sleigh bells
or an invasion of spectral creatures,
but frogs sing loud and fast only to mate.

Tiny carolers bearing dark crosses
on their backs, they remain invisible
but for sound, but for faith.

The pulsing chorus is my creed, a promise
kept yearly by this worshiping choir,
a shrill, clear, call of hope.

Fox

Watering my garden at half past six,
I watch fox run up the driveway, auburn coat
thick and glossy, fuzzy pennant of a tail.
Fox scurries across the lawn,
squeezes between rosebushes
to a burrow beneath the stone wall.

I've lived on this quarter acre
over three decades, but with senses
sharpened by hunger and procreant urgency,
fox knows my plot better, assumes
ownership by adverse possession
of deliberate and awakened necessity.

Late afternoon, I look out the window
while vacuuming. Fox lounges on the lawn,
rolls and slides like a dog, stops suddenly,
scratches, pricks up ears, looks around,
and resumes. Suddenly standing, a shake
of the head ripples down body to tail.

Science tells me of habits and habitat,
diet, and mating, diagrams internal organs
and functions. But no necropsy
or radio collar reveals fox ferocity and feral
self-possession, and I long to peer into windows
of perception closed and darkened.

At dusk, I see two pups playfully tussle
like kittens, jump, prance, collide and wrestle
on the grass. It seems like joy even
though I know from fairytales to sipping
cocktails at pickup bars, that foxes are only
sly, vicious, cunning, sneaky and sexy.

It's hard to see a fox without a mirror,
but I long for just an inkling of animal
instinct to put into a painting, song or poem.
Fox souls are stolen by human
attributes, leaving them less than they are
so we can tell stories about ourselves.

Orb Weaver

Gossamer strands roping post
to rhododendron, a spider sets up shop
on my porch, sits in a silken galaxy
of concentric threads and radiating
spokes, not knowing
what his weir in the wind will catch.

Spidery patience outlasts this lottery
of fated sticky filaments almost invisible
but for beads of morning dew,
or slanted streams of late afternoon sun.
I check the catch while sipping an early coffee,
or tilting a twilight bottle of beer.

We may fear eight legs, but time
becomes an elaborate web we weave
as years pass, a net of stranded yearnings.
How we fret over our harvest of hours,
until discovering hope's necessity
caught like insects in a latticework of dreams.

Lepidoptera Opera

for Jay Kaplan, naturalist

Names sounding as colorful
as their scale-shingled wings,
butterflies entice my eyes and ears.

checkerspot, sootywing, ringlet,
orange sulphur, painted lady,
Acadian hairstreak, dreamy duskywing

Speed dating flowers
for sweet nectar, the blossoms pale
beside these stained glass pollinators.

wood-satyr, question mark, comma,
broken-dash, wood nymph, pine elfin,
great spangled fritillary

Fragile as summer,
I watch them float lazily, drift on breezes,
flutter, zigzag, and dodge.

pearly-eye, viceroy, eyed brown,

silver-spotted skipper, pearl crescent,

eastern tailed-blue, spicebush swallowtail

Warning signals

wearing gaudy op art, they live but days or weeks

prophesizing a season of change.

silvery blue, cabbage white,

pepper and salt skipper, tortoiseshell,

red admiral, long dash, dun skipper

I feel childish

erratically running with my net,

but on the chase I won't grow old.

clouded sulphur, monarch, checkerspot

mourning cloak, bronze copper,

cloudywing, spring azure

Winged Dusk

Twilight gathers under a glowering sky,

the air a-chitter with noisy chimney swifts

that speedily circle and dart for insects as light slowly

leaks away. Cigars with wings,

their charcoal silhouettes dive and swoop

in an ever-narrowing orbit wheeling

around a rooftop, the brick chimney their axle.

The arc of swirling centripetal

motion tightens with each dizzying revolution

until all vanish in a sudden vortex of birds

spinning so quickly they seem sucked down the flue.

Pulling the last daylight behind

them like a slammed door, they leave

me dazed in earthbound darkness.

Turkey Hunting

Before first light in mid-May,
meadow grass is frosted stiff,
glowing silver under a full moon
with shadowy woods beyond.

Camouflaged head to toe,
turkey on my mind, a double
barrel side-by-side in a gloved hand,
I make for the silhouetted tangle of trees.

Stopping to get my bearings,
I spot a woodcock descending
in zigzagging spirals, softly whirring,
twittering, landing invisible

among weeds where a buzzing nasal
peent repeats like insect hum.
Rotund, short legged, with a worm
digging beak so long

you'd think he might trip over it,

he hardly looks romantic.

But the beauty of his dawn dance

forever keeps my shotgun silent.

Stars fading as I sit with my back

against an oak, the stillness

is profaned by honking geese overhead

as light sifts through unfurling greenery.

Firearm across my lap, I call with raspy

yelps and rusty clucks as the woods

come alive with chattering warblers

and a woodpecker tapping for a meal.

I call and listen, listen and call again,

disguised as a hen to lure some love

starved tom to the big lie of my gun muzzle.

Three hours and a sore back later

a gobbler responds to my lusty sounds,

the forest ringing with his guttural, wilding

cackle. And now it's call and response,

call and response as the bird walks

toward me, halts and comes closer
until it's fleshy blue head and inflamed
red wattles glow like a torch.
With loud rustling leaves from behind,

I pivot to face a coyote about to pounce
on me, an ersatz bird. Seeing
the falsehood, he brakes with a skid
of outstretched forepaws,

darting away as my sudden move
sends the gobbler to a truer love.
Undone by duplicity, I break the action,
stuff the shells in a pocket and step

onto a muddy path of deer prints
where porcupine quills mark a deathly struggle.
Powdered with soft green pollen, my boots
are accidental carriers of life.

Counting Crows

Crows stream overhead near dusk—
first in ones, twos and threes like fragments
of the oncoming dark. Soon tens arc
across the dimming sky, then hundreds
in a coal-black river of birds
seemingly driven on God's breath.

Three of us in a supermarket parking lot
count thousands, tens of thousands,
craning our necks upward in the gray
winter gloaming. Quizzical shoppers stare,
pushing carts filled with bags
of apples, steaks, and frozen pizzas.

Flying over the pavement to the far
horizon, crows land in tall skeletal trees
as thick with scuffling, shuffling,
raucous birds as it was with summer
leaves, an apartment building of branches
safe from owls, warmed by communion.

Ancient sages augured the future,
received messages by numbers, direction,
and flight of crows. East prophesized
visits by relatives, northwest by strangers,
and south presaged storms. West forecast
distant travel, and northeast fires.

We, too, peer ahead on winged
silhouettes, calling it science. Wary
that changing roosts and numbers may
foretell disease, climate change,
and the wages of urban sprawl, we seek
omens on a seesaw of hope and doubt.

VII. Quotidian Errands

What is the use of a house if you haven't got
a tolerable planet to put it on?
—*Henry David Thoreau, letter to H. G. O. Blake, May 20, 1860*

Garden

God Almighty first planted a garden.
—Francis Bacon

Bowed as if in prayer,
back-sore from pulling weeds,
fingers caked in dirt, I work
for green tomatoes, silent
daylily bells, and red
floribunda roses heavy with perfume.

Conspiracy of rain, soil, sun
and a systematic mind, my garden
is stationary but not still.
It's of the moment, moving in time
with kaleidoscopic shifting colors and shapes,
new sprouts, and fading blossoms.

Needy as a toddler, enduring cold,
drought, and insects, the garden
grows this gardener and lasts only
as long, waiting to rewild
when I'm compost at last,
resting from the work of creation.

House Painting

I scrape what's peeled and blistered
from my house,
the alligatored rind that tells time
like tree rings,
reveals stories layered in pigments—
white, dark olive, cerulean blue.

At work in warmth and fair weather,
I find a soothing tedium
in the soft rhythm of a brush on clapboards—
like music, poetry,
a pitcher's windup, waves
lapping rocky shores.

My body hangs from aluminum rungs,
but the ladder
might as well be Jacob's
as my mind climbs and wanders
to the quiet sweep of China bristles
laden with color.

Cracks, chips, and mildew are instantly hidden

by a fresh complexion.

I revel in this rain-washed deception,

a sacrament that creates home,

a Sisyphean task that will haunt,

as nothing stays new forever.

Lawn Mowing

Embraced by the mower's roar,
I find myself in deep quiet
where no sound interrupts or penetrates.

From the edge inward I ring round
an irregular labyrinth of lawn,
clipping rye, clover, fescue and Kentucky blue.

My mind wanders to the rhythm
of cyclic steps, thoughts oozing
like sweat-glossed arms in summer sunlight.

I construct grocery lists, climb Bear Mountain,
conjure notions for poems,
rehearse conversations, see my dead father.

Practical beyond reproach,
barbering the greenery lets whimsy
run riot, finds irreverent dreams in daylight.

Briggs & Stratton vibration and vroom
is my secret engine of meditation,
the sharp blade spinning like my brain.

Supermarket Magic

The same gray-haired group each week
at 6 a.m., foraging groceries on senior discount day.
We're masked in pandemic times,
learning to smile with our eyes,
muffled voices full of quibbles and quips.

I'm cruising apples and lettuce, cans of soup,
a salmon fillet, carton of eggs, bread,
quart of milk, and all the drinks and eats
sustaining life, a dull household necessity
framing hours of cooking, cleaning.

Drudgery fades as the moment folds
into so many others reaching back decades.
Rows of produce glow colors of summer, glass cases
of frozen ravioli and spinach radiate winter,
memories as well stocked as the shelves.

I drove a racecar when mom plopped
me in the shopping cart, whizzed down broad
aisles past pyramids of cans, her free hand

keeping me from grabbing colorful cereal boxes
as she sorted coupons, reached for Cheerios.

Teen buddies in tow, I stumbled into harsh light
with late night munchies, giggling,
wearing blue sunglasses, on the lookout
for parents, and snatching Oreos,
potato chips, Cokes, fumbling for change.

As a new dad, I hunted ripe bananas
and applesauce, checked cans
for salt and fat, puzzled long over tiny
Gerber jars against fickle infant tastes
for pureed carrot or turkey & gravy.

Wandering this accidental town square,
I've traded talk on the new firehouse, Red Sox
games, what the kids are up to, Cape Cod
vacations, how the knee surgery healed—
chitchat alchemized to nutrition.

I know Joe, Fred and Jen partly by peeking
into their baskets—frozen pizza, yogurt, Cheez Whiz.

I had my last conversation with Art at the deli,

his worn Yankee cap askew. A bad heart

kept him from collecting our bet on the Series.

Necessity bleeds to rhythm, births ritual

in this temple of abundance forever sheltering me

from hunger and the backache of harvest.

Grocery shopping ripens to sacrament,

memory becomes a sea anchor dragging time.

Carotid Artery

A soft spring night, mist sifting
through bare tree branches, hanging in ghostly
patches and drifting along a lonely
rain slicked road glowing under headlights.

We're pedal to the metal, geared up,
ready for anything and giddy with adrenalin,
strobes pulsing in the darkness,
sirens slicing apart the night like a scalpel.

Pavement narrows at a tight, uneven elbow
where a Volkswagen bug scraped along
a rotted guardrail, crashed through the cable
and lies crushed against an ancient oak.

Popping the door with a Halligan,
we find a boy slumped over the wheel,
the dashboard and windshield spattered bright
red, a spurt of blood to each remaining heartbeat.

We radio for paramedics, call for a chopper,

but with a cut carotid we can only

hope against all we know and watch life

leak away, wondering if we arrived too soon.

Wrapping the wound, we wait, the woods

ringing with weird rhythmic amphibian

calls, the road dotted with flattened frogs

and salamanders on a night of resurgent life.

Junk Drawer

My kitchen junk drawer
is a grab-bag of orphaned odds
and ends at the ragged edge of lost
and urgently needed.

A hungry mouth devouring whatever
I absent-mindedly toss inside,
it's a jumbled collage of scissors,
rubber bands, flashlights, batteries,
string, road maps, tape, a hammer
and pliers, old coupons,
dull pencils with worn-down erasers,
pipe cleaners, leftover screws and hex
nuts from forgotten projects,
and curious pieces of hardware
seemingly spontaneously generated.
Like Mary Poppins' carpetbag,
it has endless capacity
until it doesn't.

Why can't I find the giant
paper clips I know are in there?
I fret, as a tangled miscellany
of memories mounds on the counter
—wire I used to fix a clock,
a fridge magnet Josh made at camp,
a champagne cork from my wedding.

A packet of marigold seeds
long expired falls to the floor.
I pick it up, grab my coat and keys in frustration
as I leave to buy a box of paper clips.

I reach for the trash, but instead
sprinkle the rice-shaped
seeds in soil along the driveway.
I've nothing to lose.

Flea Market

Outcast objects from attics and basements
bake in the sun, broken fragments
of other lives, like pets
of the dead awaiting adoption.

Locks and keys, machine parts,
street signs, lamps and crockery are washed
up on the curbside of castoff commerce,
beckon in a lottery of lost belongings.

A suit like my father's hangs limp,
and the identical teakettle mother used is stranded
silent beside Tinkertoy spools and sticks
like ones I made into windmills and giraffes.

I'm a voyeur, wandering
among spinners and treble-hooked spoons
from father-son fishing trips, China
set on generations of Thanksgiving tables.

Orphaned by time, fashion and technology,
we find an afterlife for the ghosts
of other lives, adding strata of memories,
not knowing what spirits we invite home.

Carolina Rocker

A long period of hospitalization and convalescence
following a spinal operation in October, 1954,
gave me my first opportunity to do the reading
and research necessary for this project.
   —*John F. Kennedy,* Profiles in Courage

Worn down, scolded by a nagging back,

I ask what the Carolina Rocker can do for me.

Embraced in steam-bent oak and woven rattan,

I find the angle of incline and the seesaw

swing and sway eases my ache.

It's a brisk sit, like walking while seated.

I sat at my mom's skirt hem to the thump and hiss

of her ironing, as Kennedy sparred with Nixon

in jittery black-and-white. A few years later,

a shot in Dallas sent me home from school.

I saw Oswald murdered live on television

and John-John salute a flag covered casket.

I could rock endlessly in a chair that sweetened

the president's suffering. Rhythmic

motion stirs both memory and legs, pain

fires time's essence, saturates the moment

with necessity, just as distance provokes

our reach beyond profiles to full-frontal courage.

Anniversary at Equinox

—for Mary

We took vows in summer,
partied in fall,
and spliced our lives
to September's seesaw of seasons,
muggy one day, crisp the next,
moods married one to the other.

On the 22nd, a day of twos
twice blessed, we
coupled our fortunes of love
and quotidian time, making sacraments
of eating and sleeping,
sharing the blind bargains of days.

At the fulcrum of light and dark,
summer's delights flowed
into slowly unspooling autumns.
Soon, winter's cold will draw us
closer as time itself freezes,
and two are finally avowed as one.

Photographic Memory

Framed on bureaus and a desk,
fastened to walls, photos of friends,
family and far off places soaked
in living colors remind me who I am.

Daily companions, they remember
spring's layered greenery, your sapphire
eyes, and my father, young and jacked
in olive drab years before my birth.

Blues, yellows, and reds slowly bleed away
in sunlight and time fueling my
days, leaving faded prints, like cataracts
clouding the view rather than viewer.

Fugitives of memory, radiant pictures
remain lodged in my mind's camera
eye, freeze-frames of kinetic life
until in a last breath I take them with me.

Dreaming Norman Rockwell

I dream a Norman Rockwell world
where all is well and rock solid.
Let me slip into a canvas
where colors always please the eye
and the story is true and sweet.

I'm the man standing to speak
at town meeting, and the runaway
boy on a stool beside the cop at a lunch
counter. I watch a ballgame
through a fence knothole. I'm the doctor
with my stethoscope on the girl's doll,
and one of the kids shooting marbles.

We've all been there in a jumbled
déjà vu of discovery and escape,
a place where the heart paints
a little Rockwell into a reality
far beyond experience.

On Stockbridge's storybook
Main Street, the mountains Rockwell
painted behind the Red Lion's rambling
grandeur have eroded away. The line
between hopes and dreams is thin
when we crave a postcard world
we cannot put a foot through.

VIII. Neighborhood

Walking, ideally, is a state in which the mind,
the body and the world are aligned, as though they were
three characters finally in conversation together.
—*Rebecca Solnit, Wanderlust: A History of Walking*

Around the Block

Collinsville, Connecticut June 2019

How slowly can I go
tempting mystery, wonder, unexpected shadows
pooled at the edges of objects? I loiter and loaf,
time ripened to a thin, permeable membrane,
a measure of distance, as breathable as air.
On a sultry June evening I step from home
to stroll around the block, a routine of decades,
the quirky macadam streets with houses
and shops so familiar I might barely see them.
In a world increasingly abstract, walking defies
abstraction, leans into earth, trusts what is under foot.

Cradled among hills, this compact riverside village
was created for brawny, sweat drenched men bent
over blazing forges, shaping steel, grinding
razor-sharp axes, machetes, adzes, and hatchets
extending the reach of human muscle.
Back in the day, black coal smoke exhaled
success from a towering brick stack and time

ticked in triphammer heartbeats. We drowse

now in leafy suburban quiet, a soundtrack

of roaring lawn mowers, emergency sirens,

and guitar chords spilled from bars on warm

nights. A place built for work long-lost lives

within a restless compass of continual becoming.

I pass beneath a muscular sugar maple

into deep shade, trunk belly-buttoned by taphole

scars from syrup-making yesterdays.

Once I measured sunlight, temperature,

and sylvan character by the drip, drip, drip

of sap as the tree and I learned each other's

ways. Replacing disease-stricken elms

that overarched the street in fountains of leaves

and dappled sunlight, this sweet tree now

grows beyond living memory. It seems forever,

even as pendant elm branches hanging over

picket fences of the past linger

in extended photographic remembrance.

Succumbing soon to age, salt, and pavement,

sky grasping maple crowns thin, branches

break, and some summer leaves brown and curl

revealing December's architecture.

With sugaring buckets so quickly forgotten,

what saplings will succeed these giants?

We expect great things of trees.

I walk toward the white Parthenon-like church,

fluted columns, classic pediment, a descendent

of Puritan creeds housed in resurrected

pagan symmetry. Sunday's ringing clang

has called to nearby houses for almost two

centuries. When doors and windows open

against the season's warmth, choir voices

join the organ's deep vibratory buzz

turning backyard gardens to chapels,

planting and weeding into prayer.

Spiritual oasis in a nuts-and-bolts village,

generations of faith still find the intersection

of timeless and temporal in a world

of fractured metaphor where information

outstrips meaning. The church poses

questions that I, perennial doubter

too easily dismiss, the tiered bell tower

sending a skeptic's gaze upward

to nubby clouds adrift in azure heaven.

From the church parking lot where the high
school once stood over eighty years, I hear barely
inaudible voices of children. Living in a world
of echoes while feigning deafness, the past
whispers, reverie reaches an ignition point
and is suddenly visible like a flickering old-time
film. Conjured by a walking rhythm,
the long, two-story shingled building
with a central tower comes into focus,
sounds growing clearer. "Chicago,"
utters an astringent adult voice, and a girl's
soprano recites Sandburg's poem.

As I move away, words distort and dissolve
into static, like fading radio reception.
Gone longer than it existed, the school
is but the ghost of age-spotted graduation
programs and diplomas, a mirage in halftone
postcard images. Paper outlasts lumber
and stone, walking becomes more
than travel from place to place.

I descend a narrow alley between a swayback

four-bay garage once a firehouse

and a barn-like building where sod-busting

steel plows were painted post-Civil War.

Born again as a Jazz Age recreation hall

for bowling's rolling thunder and the crack

of target rifle fire, the big building had rooms

for reading newspapers, card playing,

and a ladies' parlor. Now a museum

laying away memory-grasping objects

as if they were random puzzle pieces,

it's a collective trousseau where time

stands still, imagination thickens.

No hair is cut in a Gilded Age barbershop

and the general store's pot-bellied stove

stays cold, shelves stocked with goods

that can't be bought. Farm tools, musical

instruments, and stone arrowheads freeze

time in a Mobius strip loop. Walls display

hundreds of axes and blades, some bearing exotic

names—podadera, tarpala, cavadore—
whose purposes are lost. Once harvesting crops,
constructing ships, cutting trees and brush,
tools are reduced to artifacts, time-travel
talismans within a shape-shifting structure.

Sloping toward the rail trail, the alley
stairway passes walls and foundations built
of eighteen-inch grindstones worn down
from six-foot behemoths. Eroded
from honing thousands of edges,
they found new life as steps, sign bases,
and garden ornaments.

Heroically sharp tools
sought the pole with Peary, laid tracks
across Siberia's frozen swamps. Balanced
to fit the hand, keen blades harvested
rubber, fought fires and felled trees,
fomented bloody revolutions.
But nostalgia's sweet poison forgets
the tombstone geology of atomized grit
and steel breathed by muscular grinders
leaning hard into the massive wheels

in spark showers, a high whine, and burnt
friction smell. Voices reduced to rasps,
lungs heavy in slow suffocation.

Tracks scrapped half a century, cyclists,
rollerbladers, and parents pushing strollers
stride by me where dinosaur locomotives
puffed and snorted. Walkers out for casual
views or exercise command a corridor
that once connected communities with lifelines
of passengers, coal, machine parts, lumber
and steel on strict timetables. Statistics,
maps, and sepia images are faded epitaphs
for a ground-shaking roar and rumble,
fiercely hissing steam, squeal and scrape
of metal on metal. Instead, I hear snippets
of conversation, chittering swifts circling
chimneys, and sweet bicycle bells.

The trail bridges a crumbling canal deep-
shaded by dour Norway spruce. Bullfrog
calls echo like foghorns from the dark, waxy
water freckled with bright green algae.
A great blue heron stalks fish in the shallows

where the waterway's concrete walls
have collapsed and a fallen tree trunk hosted
sunbathing turtles at noon. Nature slowly
devours a Cartesian topography contrived
to drive machinery investing humanity
with hydraulic superpowers. Ragged sumac
and poison ivy guard the shore. Admired
for cloud reflections or a frigid
day's skate, the water patiently waits.

Carried on piers, the path leads high
above the factory of redbrick and barn-board
buildings lining the river like a fortress.
A fossil teetering on the fulcrum of memory
and anticipation, structures are overgrown
with vines and trees, moldering with collapsed
roofs, spalling concrete and broken windows.
Band-aid tarps and weathered
plywood patches reveal a sad, timeserving
faith in low-contrast-light and cash.

Quiet seems unnatural in this industrial
Stonehenge from an age when shaping steel
was a way of self-knowing. So, seized

by an abiding voltage in a realm richer

in dreams than sleep, I see workers in caps

and overalls, callused hands shoveling coal,

hauling scrap in carts, their hammers

clinking on anvils, pushing blades

into the whirr and gritty whine of grind wheels,

standing in sheds stripped to the waist,

bodies sweat-glossed, placing heat-glowing steel

in pulsing coal fires before a final quenching hiss.

Too much has happened for these presences

to evaporate. Malleable, elastic time lives

in every object forged here sure as soil layers

or tree rings conjure history. But we squander

a hollowed-out inheritance built of bull-work.

Meanings exceed our grasp, grow meaningless

until only myths move us to the next place

in a world increasingly placeless

where we protect what might-be from

what-is. Waterpower and muscle conspired

to build what rainwater and neglect

slowly dissolve in a world of open wounds.

Spanning the river, the rail trail bridge

is a colossal riveted lattice of rusting struts

and girders with a Roman aqueduct's

outsized grandeur and enduring impermanence.

Built for heavy, hulking trains, it comically

dwarfs walkers and bikers. But even

in retirement, steel trusses remember the regular

heft and sway of railcars. Years fold one thing

over another in a zombied world

of unconscious contours where ruins fool

us into thinking we know a place.

Far below, the river sparkles, bares teeth

in whitewater riffles, reflects trees and a cloud

studded sky, starts gathering day's-end light

until at dusk it's the brighter element,

reflecting a neon sunset. A family picnics

on elephantine rocks, a fisherman plays

the lottery on a looping fly line,

and children swim into the current.

Both boundary and corridor dividing

and uniting, moving water's an abacus

marking millennia, continually carving

the valley with time as flow and flow as time.

River muscles turning wheels,
gears and leather belts
long sustained this place,
and now keep company with sight-seekers,
kayakers and birdwatchers. Let me
be washed and washed away, a paddler,
riparian rockhopper and flycaster.

Mesmerized by rushing water, wind-
sough, sun glitter, and summer's scent
of mucky decay, time slows, swirls back
on itself in a momentary eddy. I imagine
the river's voice trickling through me
as an eagle swoops so low I hear wingbeats,
feel a fleeting shadow, slanted late day
sun bleaching head and tail.
Once unseen for generations,
the bird fills me with whiskey warmth.
I cross more than the river.

From the bridge, I gaze upstream
at Sweetheart Mountain, forested beaver-backed
ridge of gray schist, the valley's
western wall. A ragged palisade of chestnut

oak and pine along the crest blaze

in a Kodachrome fire of last golden light,

the slopes beneath a darkling green shadow

inviting night. This rugged barometer

of resident moods shifts with the ebullience

of sun, a mercurial ghosting of snow,

or clouded melancholy. Once clearcut

to feed hungry forges with charcoal,

emergent grasses then fed cows and sheep

until trees returned and skiers tested gravity

with downhill runs and a Chevy engine rope tow.

Central Park's Olmsted scaled these slopes

as a teen, watched the curvy, glistering river,

listened to hammers echo on steel

from the factory below. He dreamed

of Nature in human nature, the proximity

of woods and water to work seeding

ideas to bloom across a nation.

On trails carved through oak,

maple and birch, I've climbed these slopes

with my children. The coarse

stone little remembers their soft hands

clambering over ledges enticing

with silvery mica sparkle.
We are mere tenants on time resistant
rock where glacial claws incised
the surface with deep memory.

Crossing the water, I follow the narrow road
upstream along the opposite bank,
pavement arcing to the river's camber.
Trees arching overhead harbor premature
darkness, fireflies twinkling like votives.
Fading trout lily, Dutchman's breeches, and trillium
bloom at roadside, soon yielding to blue-eyed
chicory, lace-topped yarrow, and plumes
of noxious bamboo-like knotweed.
Feathered goldenrod will blossom before frost
toasts the last aster and winter seals
the ground till trout lilies sprout again.

Climbing slightly, and beyond the vaulted
tree-ceiling, the road widens. To one side
rushing water, on the other orderly rows
of side-by-each worker duplexes once precisely
the same, but now cousins after almost
two-hundred-years of successive families,
technologies and fashion.

I imagine the houses
gossiping about their people—
bull-work-steam-whistle routines, laundry
on the line, stew on the stove
and interlocking inadvertent intimacies
that grew when every life was beholden
to the mill. I eavesdrop on walls talking,
hear children shouting and giggling,
men and women in cascades of laughter,
the soft, halting whimpers of tears
and groaning reverie of love.
All seems familiar and now in a place
that's hardly what it was but still looks like it.

Nearing the stout brick powerhouse
where a turbine once spun electrons feeding
factory machines, my ears pound
with an incessant, urgent roar, water
sliding over the dam and erupting to foam
in rock-strewn rapids below.
Vibrations hum like electricity in my chest.

Depression-built and abandoned decades,
a boarding house for Scandinavian

workers stood here where for centuries

the Tunxis speared and netted shad

and salmon slowed by upstream struggle.

Lost in hypnotic sound and flow,

I imagine Natives still feasting on fish,

and slide-rule-engineers descending into the turbine

pit in an Escher-like vision of paths twisting

back on each other, a 3D labyrinth

braiding disparate moments. Still, the past

casts long shadows, and with a fresh dynamo

the river will soon again do our bidding.

I recross the river on a massive mid-century

concrete and steel Interstate style highway bridge

built after flooding ripped away yesterday's

delicate twin-arched trusses.

Water tumbles over itself onto ledges,

around boulders, rapids flashing white

like shards of porcelain as they have in time

beyond bridges and history.

Reaching the far bank, I pass the Forebay,

a square pool of calm water that feeds

canals, reflects weathered, sagging buildings

where blades were forged, polished,

and painted. A belled cupola, quiet a century,

creates a photo-op remnant authenticity

made picturesque with neglect,

allows harvesting images with lenses

to trump the thing itself,

delivers a neat, curated reality.

Within the moldering structures, artists

and engineers, silk screeners, marketeers

and advertisers, therapists and woodworkers

ply their trades. Occasionally, a band's

practice shakes beams and rattles

windows with guitar riffs and drumbeats.

Above the rooftops, against the horizon,

hillside obelisks and columns, slabs

of granite and marble catch the moon's

first milky glimmer, stand like chess pieces

whose next move tests memory.

In this mirrored village, bankers, doctors,

and shopkeepers find their angle of repose

in tiered rows beside barbers, carpenters

and mechanics, silent neighbors whose remains

and names are joined to soil and slope.
Heroes lie beside suicides, the factory's
founder with machinists and blacksmiths,
stillborn babes with septuagenarians.

Energy continually circulates, a cycle of souls,
the dead a reminder that even linear
hours loop and twist, that human lifetimes
measure little where death is but a story
hidden below grass, the amnesia of the living
leaving past promises forgotten by the future.

Turning onto Main Street, I feel footfall
after footfall reverberate between buildings
in the gathering dark, each step
like the tick of a clock. The long brick
structure once packing axes
is an antique shop where ordinary objects
age into art. Conversation and laughter
pour from the old freight depot become a pub.

I'm entangled where buildings
possess both aura and architecture.
The block-long street once buzzed full

of life's necessities from medications
to hardware, clothing to groceries.
You can still get a haircut, cash
at the bank, stamps at the post office,
buy jewelry or sit down to a restaurant
meal, but yesteryear's world unto itself
has fled to malls and cyberspace.

Successive tenants inhabit old storefronts
like hermit crabs finding new shells.
Yet, old-time aproned shopkeepers linger,
anxious ghosts where what-once-was has the same
valence as what-is for those who notice stone
steps cupped by generations of feet
and the uneven topography of layered paint.

Fire-eyed Harpers Ferry Brown still stalks these streets,
and Spanish leaks from the old brick hotel
once hosting Latin machete buyers. Time is current
coursing through me, for a community
may lose its reason for being but not its past,
only its memories.

I'm comforted by skyward glances,
the unyielding order and regularity

of constellations that held stories for ancient

shepherds and shone on the factory

in its heyday. Cautionary tales

of god-favored heroes and beasts connecting

cultures over millennia, these pinpricks

of white fire may reach our eyes long

after the stars have burned away,

illuminating present and future with the past's

incandescence. Rounding the corner,

I find myself back at home where the factory

foreman and schoolteacher once lived,

where my garden, dinner and love-life await.

Who knows what rhythms walking

awakens? Sometimes the body

remembers what the mind has forgotten.

Awe outstrips analysis, time expands

to fill space channeling outward exploration within.

Like beachcombers on ebb tides,

we go back and back again, searching

for something, uncertain of what we'll find

on a hunch that salvation is in seeking.

IX. Confluences

Whatever befalls the earth befalls the sons of the earth.

—Ted Perry, Home

Frog Run

Choruses of peepers sing an endless
ringing chirp from a half-frozen swamp
beyond the sugarbush. I harvest

the last run before the sap goes sour.
For six weeks I'm a divining rod
of fickle weather, both groundhog

and shadow, the lifeblood of maples
circulating within me. Now I'm bone-sore
from a long season, pushing myself

in deep zombied exhaustion.
Thousands of gallons hauled from
trees to sugarhouse, only to drive

most of it off in frenzied boils, churning
with foam and large cauliflowered
bubbles conjuring a Zen-like trance

where less becomes so much more.
Sweet steam is my heaven-bound incense,
the shack sauna-like with moisture

and warmth, welcoming friends
out of freezing winds and early dark.
We chat away hours, the heart's

endearing trivialities opening without
warning since boiling is made
of time and listening. Clear liquid

slowly thickens to golden, an alchemy
of concentrated sunshine
ripening the sugarmaker into spring.

Trash Blossoms

The more you can throw away the more it's beautiful.
    —Arthur Miller, *The Price*

Caught at roadside in drab, ragged, early spring

grasses I find the season's brightest blooms,

incandescent even in cloud-filtered light.

Shards of blue, purple and red plastic

from broken toys and crushed bottles, windblown

cereal and cracker boxes, candy bar wrappers

and potato chip bags in colors unknown to nature

grow as sure as clover and dandelions.

Sprouting each year as snowbanks rot away, I pick

these tattered trespassers, remnants of the poverty

of plenty, for the beauty of their absence.

Sidewalk Alive

The ant's a centaur in his dragon world.
　　—Ezra Pound

Thousands of ants swirl

along a sidewalk crack, dark

mahogany bodies moving

like metal filings to a magnet.

Granular soil volcanoes

bubble up from below

where concrete secures

dry, rootless space.

I envy this certainty

of purpose, searching out

dropped ice cream cones, a stray

potato chip or cookie crumb.

As a child, I stomped.

Now, a pointillist painting

in motion stirs childlike

fascination, for a world unseen.

Paintbrush and Rifle

Lowering binoculars, I look down
at my Audubon field guide and confirm
the sighting—a golden-crowned kinglet
high in a shaggy Norway spruce.
Gazing again through the lenses,
I imagine John James Audubon peering
along the sight of his Long Tom rifle.

Silencing birds with bullets,
he made them immortal in luminous
brushstrokes, posing them so lifelike
with wires they seem to dance,
colors so vivid the images sing
loudly in whistles, trills, liquid
warbles, and harsh corvid cries.

Brand name for protecting birds,
mammals, reptiles and fish, swamps,
grasslands and mountainsides,
he taught us to see a wonderstruck
utility in beauty and forget the blood-
stained paints, the killing that saved,
enabling us to repent in his name.

Thoreau's Cairn

He's less dead than he'd ever imagined,
his simple house alchemized to an icon
by pilgrims grasping stones from home,
speaking languages from around the globe.

I longed to hear his voice, imagined
it in the wind, but only heard a kingbird's
high querulous cries. Henry was speaking,
in the only way he'd want to sound.

I placed my stone on the shape-shifting pile
of spires, plateaus and slopes, a jumble
of granite, schist, and sandstone, each piece
calling in its own tone, cadence and diction.

Life on Stone

Obscuring the cemetery's trove
of names, dates and clichéd phrases,
crusty leaflike lichens spread in warty
starbursts and crinkled slatey-green rosettes.

Erasing time and memory, they slowly
devour stone with acetic secretions, patiently
transforming granite and gneiss to soil
as sure as earth reclaims caskets and bones.

Coarse but delicate, living centuries,
steady, persistent growth straddles
the years between human life and eternity,
defying hopes for perpetual care.

Spring in the Ancient Burying Ground

So much life

in this subdivision of the dead.

Grass grows long, thickens and greens,

dotted with buttercups, dandelions,

and bluets that draw softly humming bees.

Teakettle calls of Carolina wrens echo

down the somber rows.

A mockingbird scolds atop an obelisk

as a woodchuck scurries to its burrow.

And as you read the fate of me,
Think on the glass that runs for thee.

Soul effigies peer

eerily, wings outstretched or upswept.

They watch and follow as I pass, faces

broad or narrow with smiles or frowns,

eyes wide or closed, noses thin

or bulbous, hair wavy or straight.

Is character visible,

or just the artistic skill that sculpted

spirals, loops and rosettes?

To worms and reptiles made prey
Shall rise and shine at the great day.

Chiseled words speak
for the silent, names and dates
embalming a moment, connecting
me to distant worlds.
Octogenarians lie beside infants,
and Revolutionary War soldiers, drowning
and smallpox victims are near
mothers who agonized in childbirth.
Their rhyming couplets sing warnings.

Stop kind reader and drop a tear
on this cold dust that slumbers here.

Lichen splotches obscure
inscriptions, brownstone flakes,
marble darkens and melts,
schist and slate erode erasing memory.
No longer frozen in the legible
afterlife of the living, perhaps spirits

now freely ascend, leaving behind

those weighted by large,

elaborate monuments in perpetual care.

As I am now so you must be

Prepare for death and follow me.

Breezes are breath

of the dead, their voices in birdsong,

a lasting presence in stars and sunshine.

Opening a gate, I squeeze

through a crack in time,

blessed to wander in eternity

and walk out, shoes dusted

with yellowish pollen, spreading life

from a land of the long dead.

Cicadas at Sixty

Let me go out to cicada songs,
and ripen to compost for tree roots
where the cyclical insects feed.

Clouds of chorusing for my street parade,
sonic declarations of dust and ash,
an inscrutable vibratory rhythm
like the throaty hum of Tibetan monks.

Trumpeting the very pulse of time,
they emerge from earthy blackness
ready for music, sex and revelry.

Grant me that next seventeen
years, the luck of sevens twice,
for a selfsame celebration
before my own stay in darkness.

Finding Heaven

Forget angels plucking harps in cumulus
mist, bluegrass with banjos
and mandolins will enliven my afterlife.

Skip ascent skyward, let my soul walk
in mossy woods among towering oaks and pines
where brooks chatter in rocky tumbles.

My afterworld is an ancient tavern alive
with conversation and laugher,
a cold amber ale and plate of fish and chips.

Maybe heaven can wait, since lives
like mine are short, and life is endless
at an imperfect paradise not far away.

Instructions for a Funeral

Burn me down and carry me up
to the heights where my soul soared
when two legs could muscle
their way to ledgy outcrops
looking toward distant hills.
Release to the breeze what fire
can't devour, float it among branches
of oak, yellow birch, and hemlock
to settle in humus where roots will find me.

Cast a handful like bread
on the Farmington to float by familiar
trees, farms, hills, factories
and homes, a last goodbye
before reaching seawater
where I'll dissolve in an ocean
that birthed life
and to which all things terrestrial return.

Forget flowers until spring
when forest ephemerals arise in margins
of warming sun and unfurling leaves.

In the woods and air you will find me

among hepatica's delicate pink

abloom in a last snow, and as fiddleheads

unwind beside nodding bells of trout

lily and feathery leaves of squirrel corn.

I'll be there, always, to refresh your spirit.

about the author

David K. Leff is an award-winning poet and essayist, and former deputy commissioner of the Connecticut Department of Environmental Protection. He is the Canton, Connecticut poet laureate, deputy town historian, and town meeting moderator. He was a volunteer firefighter for 26 years.

In 2016 and 2017 David was appointed by the National Park Service to serve as poet-in-residence for the New England National Scenic Trail (NET). He has been nominated three times for a Pushcart Prize, and has twice been a finalist in the Connecticut Book Awards. David has received two silver medals from the Independent Publisher Book Awards (IPPY), and was grand prize short-listed for the Eric Hoffer Book Award. His work has appeared in anthologies, newspapers such as the *Hartford Courant,* and magazines including *Appalachia* and *Yankee.*

The author of seven nonfiction books, three volumes of poetry, and two novels in verse, David's work focuses on the connection of people to their communities and the natural environment. He often explores commonplace elements of the world around us that have hidden meanings and unusual links to each other.

David has been the book review editor of *Connecticut Woodlands,* the quarterly magazine of the Connecticut Forest & Park Association and is now poetry editor. He is a staff writer for *The Wayfarer Magazine.*

David's papers are located at the
Special Collections and University Archives, UMass/Amherst.
View his work at www.davidkleff.com

HOMEBOUND
PUBLICATIONS

Since 2011 We are an award-winning independent publisher striving to ensure that the mainstream is not the only stream. More than a company, we are a community of writers and readers exploring the larger questions we face as a global village. It is our intention to preserve contemplative storytelling. We publish full-length introspective works of creative non-fiction, literary fiction, and poetry.

Look for Our Imprints Little Bound Books, Owl House Books, *The Wayfarer Magazine*, Wayfarer Books & Navigator Graphics

WWW.HOMEBOUNDPUBLICATIONS.COM

WAYFARER

BASED IN THE BERKSHIRE MOUNTAINS, MASS.

The Wayfarer Magazine. Since 2012, *The Wayfarer* has been offering literature, interviews, and art with the intention to inspires our readers, enrich their lives, and highlight the power for agency and change-making that each individual holds. By our definition, a wayfarer is one whose inner-compass is ever-oriented to truth, wisdom, healing, and beauty in their own wandering. *The Wayfarer's* mission as a publication is to foster a community of contemplative voices and provide readers with resources and perspectives that support them in their own journey.

Wayfarer Books is our newest imprint! After nearly 10 years in print, *The Wayfarer Magazine* is branching out from our magazine to become a full-fledged publishing house offering full-length works of eco-literature!

Wayfarer Farm & Retreat is our latest endeavor, springing up the Berkshire Mountains of Massachusetts. Set to open to the public in 2024, the 15 acre retreat will offer workshops, farm-to-table dinners, off-grid retreat cabins, and artist residencies.

WWW.WAYFARERBOOKS.ORG